# My Beautiful BODY

## Carly Rowena

ILLUSTRATED BY
## Alf & Florence

Copyright 2021 by Carly Rowena | Published by Carly Rowena | Illustrations by Alf & Florence
ISBN: 978-1-7398125-0-8

"Let us always be toddlers who strut with our bellies forward"

To Jax, always be you.

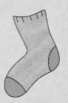

I found it

underneath

my clothes,

and in my wellies
where I wriggle my toes.

It loves to dance

and

<u>jump</u> and crawl,

And lets me grow from
small to tall.

It loves to make noises that
make me giggle,

I can
toot-toot
from my
butt-butt,

And
snort
when I
sniffle.

It comes in all colours and sizes and shapes,

And loves to eat everything,

especially <u>cakes</u>.

We play with our food,

the bath and our toys,

And <u>stomp</u> like a dinosaur

and make lots of noise.

My beautiful body is my

best friend to keep,

It never leaves me lonely

and is there while I sleep.

Together for adventures like
<u>jumping</u> in puddles,

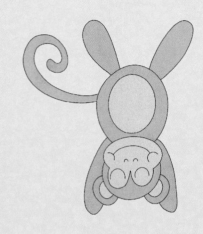

No matter what happens,

we'll always have cuddles.

My beautiful body,

my own little home,

I promise to love you
and together we'll roam.

# Carly Rowena

Carly is the writer behind this book, she loves reading to her daughter Jax so much that she wanted to create her own book that would have you falling in love with how beautiful you are, inside and out. Carly loves the glitter over the ocean but hates celery!

@carlyrowena

# Alf & Florence

Alex Jones is the illustrator behind Alf & Florence and had so much fun drawing this book. She loves drawing self affirming happy illustrations of people and animals. She loves a warm bubble bath but hates spiders!

@alfandflorence

Made in the USA
Las Vegas, NV
23 November 2021

35042312R00024